W9-BTZ-569

The Amazing Hairstyles Book

By Mari Martin

The Child's World®
www.childsworld.com

Published in the United States of America by The Child's World®
1980 Lookout Drive • Mankato, MN 56003-1705
800-599-READ • www.childsworld.com

ACKNOWLEDGMENTS

The Child's World®: Mary Berendes, Publishing Director

Produced by Shoreline Publishing Group LLC
President / Editorial Director: James Buckley, Jr.
Designer: Tom Carling, carlingdesign.com
Cover Art: Slimfilms
Assistant Editor: Jim Gigliotti

Photo Credits:
Cover: Main: iStock; insets: Dreamstime.com
Interior: AP/Wide World: 13, 19, Corbis: 5, 6, 9, 10 top;
Dreamstime.com (photographers listed): 20, Manu Conic 15, 24,
Tamora Kulikova 7, Gino Santa Maria 12, Tatjana Strelkova 21;
Getty Images: 10 bottom, 11; iStock: 8, 14, 18, 26, 27; Photos.com:
4, 16-17, 23, 25.

LIBRARY OF CONGRESS CATALOG-IN-PUBLICATION DATA

Martin, Mari, 1967-
  The amazing hairstyles book / by Mari Martin.
      p. cm. — (Reading rocks!)
  Includes bibliographical references and index.
  ISBN 978-1-60253-093-5 (library bound : alk. paper)
  1. Hairdressing—Juvenile literature. I. Title. II. Series.

TT972.M272 2008
646.7'24—dc22

2008004486

CONTENTS

THE STORY OF Hair

From keeping us warm to keeping up with fashion, hair has a long and interesting history. Hairstyles and hair care have always been a part of being human. Your hair is one of the first things that people notice about you. It helps make you the unique person you are. Is your hair curly? Straight? Short? Long? Red? Blond?

Brown? Black? What is hair exactly? Hair is made of stuff called **keratin**. Believe it or not, keratin also forms your fingernails! Hair forms under the skin in tiny pits called **follicles**. A strand of hair grows out of each follicle and up through your skin.

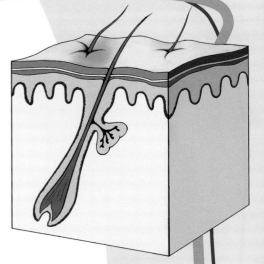

This drawing shows how a hair grows in a follicle and up through the skin.

Human head hair grows about a half an inch (1 cm) a month. If you don't cut it, it can grow up to three feet (1 m) in length—or more! You lose about 100 hairs from your **scalp** every day. But don't worry, the average person has almost 90,000 hair follicles on her head . . . and five million on her body! That's a lot of hair!

In **prehistoric** times, hair had one purpose: to keep us warm. Early humans had thick hair that covered most of their bodies. Scientists think humans probably lost this hair as they **evolved** over thousands of years. During the Ice Age (about 10,000 years ago), they probably began wearing animal skins to keep their less-hairy bodies warm.

Thousands of years later, styling head hair began to be a fashion statement. For instance, more than 4,000 years ago, hairstyles and hair care were a big deal in ancient Egypt. Egyptian men wore their

This statue shows what scientists think early humans might have looked like and what they might have worn.

hair short, or shaved their heads and wore thick wigs. Women wore **elaborate** headdresses.

Women wore wigs over their hair, too. Wigs were made from plant materials or human hair. Women also attached cones of heavily perfumed beeswax to their heads. The cones melted in the hot sun. This left their hair sweet-smelling and soft. Some Egyptians also dyed their hair red with plant juices. Ancient Egyptians were the first people to make shampoo, too. They used water, plants, and even animal fats to clean their hair.

This painting from ancient Egypt shows one of the colorful ways women styled their hair.

7

Years later, royal people in ancient Persia (where Iran is today) dusted and decorated their hair with gold and silver.

Ancient Greeks and Romans wore their hair in very fancy styles. Often, the hair was piled high on the tops of their heads. People also wove things such as ribbons, gold, and flowers into their hair.

This statue shows a typical hairstyle worn by an ancient Roman woman.

In Asia, Japanese women added beautiful pins and combs. Chinese and Indian women styled their hair with different braids and knots.

Native Americans wore their hair in many different styles. Perhaps the most famous was the Mohawk.

Men from the Iroquois nation shaved their heads on the sides and grew the hair longer on top.

In Europe in the 1600s, powdered wigs were all the rage. These headdresses were sometimes more than two feet (61 cm) tall and were made with lard and clay. They were decorated with combs, miniature ships, or even horse carriages.

Feathers were also a popular way for French women to decorate their hair.

Straight hair cut in a "bob" was inspired by movie stars.

In the United States, most women wore their hair long until the early 1900s. But then short hair became popular. Movie stars of the 1920s and 1930s started wearing their hair in short "bobs" (a haircut just below the ears). Women also started to work outside of the house more often. Shorter hair took less time to care for.

The beehive was created with hairspray and was popular in the 1950s.

Hairspray was invented in 1948. This sticky stuff can hold hair in place for hours. In the

1950s and early 1960s, women often used a lot of hairspray to keep fancy hairstyles (such as the beehive) in place.

The **permanent**, or "perm," was another style that became popular over the years. With early perms, chemicals were applied to hair. Then the hair was wrapped around tiny curlers, and women would sit underneath large hair dryers for hours! When a "home permanent" kit was introduced later on, it was a big hit. It was easy to do, and it took less time. Women could get a perm much more easily.

Women brought something to read when they got their "perms." It could take hours!

Hairstyles kept changing, however. By the late 1960s, long hair started coming back into fashion. In the 1970s and 1980s, a type of music called "punk" became popular. People who liked punk bands often colored their hair in wild shades of pink, purple, yellow, or blue. Sometimes they molded it into spikes or just shaved it all off!

Today's hairstyles aren't quite as wild. Boys are inspired by longer-haired skateboard stars, while girls often look to celebrities such as Miley Cyrus, who plays Hannah Montana. Hairstyles still play a big part in the fashion world, too.

ALL ABOUT
Hair Care

Long ago, haircuts were probably done using sharp rocks. Over time, people developed special tools for cutting hair. Some people became good at cutting hair. They became the first **barbers**.

For many years, most men went to a barbershop to get their hair cut. The men usually got very short cuts and didn't need fancy treatments. Barbers are pretty rare these days, however. Hairstylists working at **salons** get most of the business today for both men and women.

Salons can be fancy or simple, large or small. They might include a place to get your nails done, or even get a **massage**. Chances are if you've ever had your hair cut, you've been to a hair salon.

Have you ever had a neck rub? That's a type of massage, which means using your hands to rub muscles to soothe or relax them.

Experts at hair salons use scissors, hair dryers, clippers, and other tools.

When you go to a salon, have a good idea of what you want your hair to look like. You might want to bring a picture of the haircut you want. You can look through fashion magazines for ideas. Talk with your hairstylist and explain exactly how you want your hair to look.

A special sink with space to rest your neck makes washing your hair easy.

First, your stylist will wash your hair in a special sink. You get to tilt back in a comfy chair and relax.

Most stylists like to cut hair while it's wet. They use their fingers to hold the hair while they snip it.

The stylist will then lightly dry your hair and take you to another area in the salon. Then the stylist will comb your hair and use different tools such as scissors, clippers, and even razors to cut it.

When the cut is finished, the stylist will blow-dry and style your hair. Pay attention to how the stylist does this. That way, you can style your hair the same way at home, even without an expert's help!

The best part about a visit to a salon? Checking out your cool new look!

Some hairstylists become famous for the styles they create. They can also become famous for inventing hair-care products. One of the most famous hairstylists was Vidal Sassoon. Before Sassoon, the most common hair-care products were shampoo, conditioner, and

Using different types of hair products can be fun!

Inspired by Stars

Entertainers have been hairstyle-setters for years. When 1950s movie star Marilyn Monroe dyed her hair platinum blond, other women followed. More recently, Jennifer Aniston from the TV show *Friends* wore her hair in a **layered** cut. Women flocked to salons asking for "The Rachel," named for Jennifer's TV character. Long, layered hair is very popular today, thanks to beautiful actresses such as Angelina Jolie.

hairspray. Sassoon created many new products to clean, soften, and hold hairstyles.

Sassoon and other stylists brought us **mousse** [MOOSE], gels, and anti-frizz sprays. Stylists also began creating new styling tools. These included new kinds of curling irons, brushes, and even hair dryers.

A style of hair called dreadlocks turns hair into long, tight curls.

People use different products to care for different kinds of hair. People with thick or curly hair might use products to smooth it down. On the other hand, people with very straight hair sometimes want to make it curly. People with very **fine** or very oily hair might use products that make their hair thicker and bouncier.

Some products are used to change hair color. You can turn brown hair into blond, or add highlights (light streaks) to dark hair. You can even get wild colors like blue or dark red.

Stylists work with all types of hair to create the "look" that a person wants. Whatever type of hair you have, there are products and styles that are perfect for you.

In 1906, Madam C. J. Walker became the first African-American female millionaire. She created a line of hair-care products for black consumers.

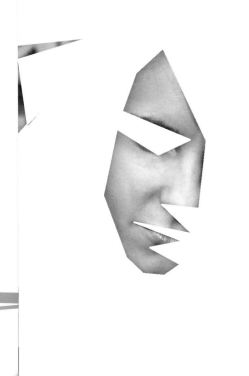

Some people like to dye their hair bold colors. Red is a popular shade.

CREATING COOL Hairstyles

With all the hair products that are available today, it can be hard to decide what's best for your type of hair. Taking good care of your hair is important, and it's also very easy to do. First, you need to figure out whether your hair is greasy or dry, thick or fine.

Here's a quick way to find out about your hair. Thread a strand of your hair through a needle. If it slides right through, it's probably fine and straight. If you have trouble, it's probably curly.

Next, drop the hair in a glass of water. If the hair floats, it's either healthy or a bit oily (because water and oil don't mix). If it sinks to the bottom, it is dry (the hair absorbed the water and sank).

Dry and curly hair can be styled into a fun and bouncy look.

One of the most important things about caring for your hair is keeping it clean.

First, find a shampoo and conditioner that matches your type of hair. Some people wash their hair every day, but you may not need to. If your type of hair is dry, washing your hair every other day is best.

You should never brush your hair while it's wet—a brush can cause wet hair to break. Instead, use a comb on wet hair.

Brushing hair while it's dry helps keep it smooth and free of tangles.

Blow . . . or no

The first hair dryers were actually vacuum cleaners! In the early 1900s, women used vacuums to pull the water from their hair.

Hair dryers called "blow-dryers" were first made in 1920. Early versions were large, but over time they became smaller. By the 1970s, dryers were the handheld types used today.

Some people use hair dryers every day. This can actually damage your hair. If you use a hair dryer often, make sure to keep your hair moisturized and healthy with a good conditioner. Be careful when using your hair dryer. Never, ever use a hair dryer around water.

Adding products such as gels or mousse can help make your hair easier to care for, too. These products can tame frizz and sometimes keep your hair from tangling.

A French braid is created by pulling sections of hair into one main braid.

Maybe you'd like to try a new look, but don't want to cut your hair. Don't worry, we've got some ideas!

Braids are a popular and easy way of changing your style. You can do a simple braid, a French braid, or maybe even cornrows (lots of little braids in rows on the top of your head). You might even want to weave some ribbons into your hair for fun.

You can try the Mohawk look by slicking down the sides of your hair with a sticky styling product such as gel or wax. Then bring the center part of your hair up into a peak. Be sure to wash the sticky products off your hands when you're done creating your Mohawk!

For fun, you can try colored hairspray. Some sprays even have glitter! And when you want to change your color back, all you have to do is wash your hair.

Changing your hairstyle is easy to do. It makes for a whole new you!

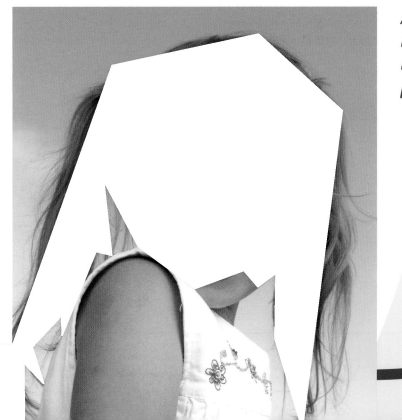

A new look can be as easy as using colorful ponytail bands.

Here's one fun way to combine all this great hair info—have a hairstyling sleepover! Take turns washing, conditioning, and rinsing your hair. Towel it dry and then . . . have fun! Trade off making fancy braids. Experiment with gels or mousse. (Who can make the highest hairstyle? Who can make the wildest shapes?) You may want to give each other a head or scalp massage, too. It feels great!

If you have straight hair, why not try a night of rag curls? Cut a clean rag into thin strips. Roll your slightly damp, clean hair into a curl around the cloth, and tie the cloth tight into a small bow. Keep the bows in overnight. The next morning, untie each rag. Presto! A head full of curls!

Whether you have long, short, thick, fine, curly, or straight hair, you can have fun with it. Take care of it, too . . . your hair is a part of you!

You can also use plastic curlers to create hairstyles. Fixing up your friends' hair can be fun and creative!

29

GLOSSARY

barbers people who cut or style hair

elaborate something that takes great care or planning or that has lots of details

evolved gradually developed

fine in hair, extremely thin

follicles small sacs or glands

keratin a protein that forms hair

layered a hairstyle in which the hair has been cut at many different lengths.

massage rubbing muscles to soothe and relax them

mousse a foamy product that helps hair stay in place

permanent a long-lasting hairstyle of waves or curls created by chemicals

prehistoric referring to a time before recorded history

salons places that offer a specific product or service; in this case, hair care

scalp the skin on top of your head

FIND OUT MORE

BOOKS

Hair (World Show and Tell)
(Two-Can Publishing, 2006)
See how children in other parts of the world wear their hair.

Hair: Styling Tips and Tricks for Girls
by Jim Jordan (Illustrator) (American Girl, 2000)
Styling tips for young girls who like to do their own hair.

Hair Trix for Cool Chix: The Real Girl's Guide to Great Hair
by Leanne Warrick (Watson-Guptill, 2004)
Lots of hair-care tips with colorful and fun illustrations.

WEB SITES

Visit our Web site for lots of links about hairstyles and hair care:
www.childsworld.com/links

Note to Parents, Teachers, and Librarians: We routinely check our Web links to make sure they're safe, active sites—so encourage your readers to check them out!

INDEX

MARI MARTIN has very long, brown hair and loves to use all kinds of hair products. Her first haircut was called the "Pixie,' which she got when she was nine years old. Mari is a children's librarian and a professional singer. She lives in Santa Barbara, California.